D0757639

R CUTE!

Monkeys

by Kari Schuetz

BELLWETHER MEDIA • MINNEAPOLIS, MN

Note to Librarians, Teachers, and Parents:

Blastoff! Readers are carefully developed by literacy experts and combine standards-based content with developmentally appropriate text.

Level 1 provides the most support through repetition of high-frequency words, light text, predictable sentence patterns, and strong visual support.

Level 2 offers early readers a bit more challenge through varied simple sentences, increased text load, and less repetition of high-frequency words.

Level 3 advances early-fluent readers toward fluency through increased text and concept load, less reliance on visuals, longer sentences, and more literary language.

Level 4 builds reading stamina by providing more text per page, increased use of punctuation, greater variation in sentence patterns, and increasingly challenging vocabulary.

Level 5 encourages children to move from "learning to read" to "reading to learn" by providing even more text, varied writing styles, and less familiar topics.

Whichever book is right for your reader, Blastoff! Readers are the perfect books to build confidence and encourage a love of reading that will last a lifetime!

This edition first published in 2014 by Bellwether Media, Inc.

No part of this publication may be reproduced in whole or in part without written permission of the publisher. For information regarding permission, write to Bellwether Media, Inc., Attention: Permissions Department, 5357 Penn Avenue South, Minneapolis, MN 55419.

Library of Congress Cataloging-in-Publication Data

Schuetz, Kari.
 Baby monkeys / by Kari Schuetz.
   p. cm. – (Blastoff! readers. Super cute!)
Audience: K to grade 3.
Summary: "Developed by literacy experts for students in kindergarten through grade three, this book introduces baby monkeys to young readers through leveled text and related photos"– Provided by publisher.
Includes bibliographical references and index.
ISBN 978-1-60014-929-0 (hardcover : alk. paper)
1. Monkeys–Infancy–Juvenile literature. I. Title.
QL737.P9S338 2014
599.8'139–dc23
                                                                    2013004880

Printed in the United States of America, North Mankato, MN.

Table of Contents

Monkey Infant!

A baby monkey is called an infant.

Life With Mom

An infant **clings** to its mom's body. It loves hugs.

It drinks mom's milk to grow strong. Soon it eats fruits.

Mom **grooms** her infant. She picks through its messy hair.

A Busy Baby

An infant stays busy. It plays with other babies in the **troop**.

It also climbs trees.
The infant moves
from branch
to branch.

The infant travels with the troop. Mom or dad gives it a ride.

Naptime

It is naptime when the troop stops. The infant sucks on its thumb.

Then it
falls asleep.
Sweet dreams,
little monkey!

Glossary

clings—hangs on tight and close

grooms—cleans

troop—a group of monkeys that live together

To Learn More

AT THE LIBRARY

Hewett, Joan. *A Monkey Baby Grows Up.* Minneapolis, Minn.: Carolrhoda Books, 2004.

Kalman, Bobbie. *Baby Lemurs.* New York, N.Y.: Crabtree Pub., 2011.

Schindel, John. *Busy Monkeys.* Berkeley, Calif.: Tricycle Press, 2002.

ON THE WEB

Learning more about monkeys is as easy as 1, 2, 3.

1. Go to www.factsurfer.com.

2. Enter "monkeys" into the search box.

3. Click the "Surf" button and you will see a list of related Web sites.

With factsurfer.com, finding more information is just a click away.

Index

The images in this book are reproduced through the courtesy of: Rattanapatphoto, front cover, pp. 14-15; Juniors Bildarchiv/ Glow Images, pp. 4-5; J & C Sohns/ Glow Images, pp. 6-7; Simone van den Berg, pp. 8-9; Yukihiro Fukuda/ Nature Picture Library, pp. 10-11, 12-13; Kathmanduphotog, pp. 16-17; Yummyyui, pp. 18-19; Eric Gevaert, pp. 20-21.